UNSOLVED **MYSTERIES**

the secret files

Yeti, the Abominable Snowman

Laura Anne Gilman

the rosen publishing group's
rosen
central

For Josepha Sherman, of course. And Loren Coleman.

Published in 2002 by The Rosen Publishing Group, Inc.
29 East 21st Street, New York, NY 10010

Copyright © 2002 by The Rosen Publishing Group, Inc.

First Edition

Library of Congress Cataloging-in-Publication Data

Gilman, Laura Anne.
Yeti, the abominable snowman / Laura Anne Gilman.—1st ed.
p. cm.—(Unsolved mysteries)
Includes bibliographical references and index.
ISBN 0-8239-3565-5
1. Yeti. I. Title. II. Unsolved mysteries (Rosen Publishing Group)
QL89.2.Y4 G55 2001
001.944—dc21

2001004514

Manufactured in the United States of America

Contents

No Yeti has ever been photographed. This artist's drawing comes from descriptions of people who claim they came into contact with the fabled mountain beast.

1

The Origins of the Yeti

"It was a creature not much taller than a man, but broader in the shoulders, and covered with heavy white hair. It walked upright, but lurched forward in all, a most terrifying sight."

—Anonymous quote

Also known as the Abominable Snowman, the Yeti is a creature of legend and conjecture, a giant ape-creature living in the snowy waste of the Himalaya Mountains. Still, it is generally accepted by scientists and folklorists alike that myths and legends often arise from at least a germ of fact. For instance, the Greek myth of the centaur, said to be half man and half horse, may have been started when someone saw a horse and rider for the first time. The person may have gotten so excited by the novel sight that he didn't know what he'd seen and told everyone he'd seen a

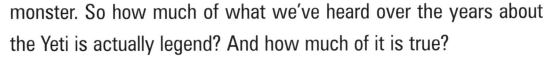

monster. So how much of what we've heard over the years about the Yeti is actually legend? And how much of it is true?

To discover what might lie under the decades of myth, hoax, and folklore, we must first understand the landscape from which the Yeti comes.

THE YETI'S WORLD

The word "Yeti" has been attributed to several sources. Some claim that it comes from the Tibetan words *Yah,* meaning "rock," and *Teh,* meaning "animal"—combining to form "rock animal," perhaps for the Yeti's resemblance to a huge snow-covered boulder. Other sources say that it is from the word for "magical creature," which it must have seemed to be to the local peoples who live in the foothills of the Himalayas.

The Himalaya Mountains, the highest range on Earth, which run along the border between India, Nepal, and Tibet, have been referred to as the roof of the world. This is a place so distant and mysterious that it seems to be not of this earth—exotic, dangerous, and, to many people, of great spiritual significance. Much of the remote and forbidding land around these rough peaks is uninhabited.

Early accounts and legends say that the Yeti roamed the Himalaya Mountains, the highest mountain range on Earth.

The tallest mountain in the world, Mount Everest, which is 29,028 feet high and lies half in Nepal and half in Tibet, is part of the Himalayas. It has given many of us a mental picture of the region as nothing but snow-capped mountains dotted with intrepid climbers fighting the elements in the name of exploration and adventure.

But there is much more to the land than that. What many people in the West don't realize is that the mountains foster a wide range of vegetation, from shrub to grazing lands to some truly impressive forests. All these lands host a wide range of animal life.

In fact, the forested areas are the home of tigers and leopards, wild ox, deer and buffalo, and the occasional elephant. South-central Nepal is one of the last homes of the great Indian rhinoceros, now protected from poaching by the government.

There are fewer wild animals in the central zone because of the clearing of forests by villagers. A few leopards, bears, and smaller carnivores inhabit the forests and ravines, and small deer are found in the woods. In the alpine zone are musk deer, goats, and wild sheep, which are the prey of wolves and snow leopards. It is there that strange tracks are often found in the snow, possibly —but not certainly—made by bears. Or are they made by the Yeti?

This is a land that was relatively untouched by modern civilization well into the twentieth century—a mysterious place uncharted by and unknown to outsiders.

A QUICK HISTORY

As far back as we know, the Himalaya Mountains were never a place of heavily populated villages or towns. In the days before "modern" conveniences such as electricity and telephone lines, people were even more isolated. The ability to travel any distance was severely limited, even with the use of the tough ponies that could live off those lands. Archaeological expeditions suggest that people lived in small family groups, centered around the herds of goats or sheep upon which they depended for milk, meat, and fur.

But even the most isolated areas of the world are subject to the migrations of people and ideas. The first real knowledge we have of the history of this area dates back to 800 BC, when the Kirat dynasty ruled Tibet. It was also during this time that Buddhism—brought from India by traveling monks, traders, and scholars to the royal court—came to the foothills of the Himalayas.

After AD 300, more people began traveling from neighboring India to Tibet. They brought with them a more sophisticated culture of record keeping and the minting of money. They also brought their religion, Hinduism. This was a time when architecture and decorative arts such as sculpture flourished in the Himalayas. In short, the society had time for leisure.

In the thirteenth century, British traders and explorers arrived in China and India, and Western influences began to creep in. Once in the area, the British never quite went home again, and in 1600 the British East India Company was created in order to simplify

trade with India. One hundred and fifty years later, the British East India Company had grown to the point where it was, in effect, running the day-to-day governance of India.

But even then, with the British in charge, the Himalayas remained relatively untouched, both because they were too difficult to explore and because there was little in the region that was of financial interest to England. The locals were hired as guides and trackers, but the land itself was still a mystery.

Today, the inhabitants are more connected to the rest of the world, thanks to modern means of communication. But the region still remains a place set apart, separated from the rest of the world by a combination of geography, politics, and climate. The local people there today are the Sherpas, who originated in Tibet, having migrated over the mountains to Nepal about five centuries ago. The Sherpas were originally farmers, herders, and traders. When the Western explorers arrived, Sherpa hunters became their guides and earned a well-deserved, worldwide reputation for their mountaineering abilities. Sherpa guides are mentioned in almost every historical account of attempts to climb Mount Everest.

It was from these people, and other local groups, that the West first encountered stories of the fabled and rarely seen Metch-Kangmi. This is another name for the Yeti. The literal translation is "repugnant snowman." It was renamed Abominable Snowman by a London reporter who sneered at the idea.

The Mythology of the Yeti

How long has the Yeti been known to the people of the Himalayas? It is almost impossible to tell when the first report of these man-beasts was made. Certainly, long before any Western observer came to Tibet or Nepal, the Yeti was already an established part of the local culture. Whether called Yeh-ti, Nyalmo, Alma, Teh-lma or Kra-dhan, and no matter how the descriptions differed—the color of the hair or how much of the creature's body it covered—all the stories agreed: The creature walked upright, had huge feet, was the size of a man but much broader, and had hair covering most of its body. And it shied away from human interaction. The occasional traveler or hunter might encounter huge footprints in the snow or lose a goat under suspicious circumstances, but actual encounters were few and far between. There were, of course, claims that a Yeti—or packs of them—had damaged villages or towns, typically looking for food.

Sherpas, the modern-day inhabitants of the Himalaya Mountains, are renowned for their mountaineering abilities and often serve as guides for Westerners.

And yet if you asked a local, he or she would be the first to assure you that these were no mere beasts. Yetis serve a purpose, they would tell you, more than any wild animal roaming for food and shelter.

In fact, according to one Sherpa legend, the Yeti were mysterious creatures who inhabited the slopes of the Himalayas, standing between mankind and the unattainable peaks of the mountains where demon-spirits lived. As such, they were beings to be wary of but not actively feared.

Anyone who claimed they'd had an encounter told of it in great detail, until the event quickly passed into legend the way an unusual or terrifying experience—such as a near miss with death—might among your friends and family today. A person's reality during moments of quick or terrifying events is altered just enough (or vastly) to be different from the truth of the event. Then, in tellings to friends and family, facts become distorted: People and objects become larger and scarier; actions become more outlandish, vivid, and deadly. After time and many more tellings, each of the people, objects, and actions in the event seem to become even more dramatic. Thus a legend is made out of an event that was not so dramatic after all. In short, there was no way to determine what was the truth of these stories, what had been embellished over the years, and what was outright creation.

The Yeti legend is much the same. Even physical evidence is not clear-cut. Many Buddhist lamaseries—homes to religious figures called lamas, much as monasteries would house monks—claimed to have relics, or religious objects, that came from the Yeti. Shamanistic relics of these sorts were used to remind Buddhists of their connection to the world around them, both in physical and spiritual terms. And, as such, stories would grow around these objects, both true and invented, in order to enhance their religious significance.

This is where the tradition of folklore comes from: the stretching of what might be or might have been into genuine storytelling. It is the job of the researcher to discover what among those stories is a verified encounter and what is myth, legend, or outright falsehood. David Gordon, author of *Field Guide to the Sasquatch,* wrote, "The absence of evidence is not necessarily evidence of an absence." In other words, lack of proof is no proof at all. The burden rests on both sides—believer and skeptic—to establish their cases.

A GLOBAL CONSPIRACY?

Although the Yeti is perhaps the best known of all such ape-man creatures, there have been related phenomena all over the world.

In the United States, we have the aptly named Bigfoot, or Sasquatch. The American ape-creature is to be found—at least according to the stories—in many states, from Florida up to the Canadian border, but the best-known stomping grounds are the woods of Washington State, where its legend first grew.

Sightings of a huge "ape-man," similar to the Yeti in both physical attributes and behavioral characteristics, have been reported around the world.

But the "ape man" is a familiar figure in folklore—both traditional and modern—all around the world. You could start as far back as ancient Sumeria and the story of Gilgamesh, whose companion Enkidu was a "wild man" who had to be taught human speech. Or you could pick up the pages of the *National Enquirer* or similar magazines and read about the latest sightings in the Pacific Northwest.

Similar sightings are everywhere. In Malaysia, eighteen-inch footprints made by a creature with a twelve-foot stride were recorded in August 1966, feeding rumors of a huge ape-man living deep within the jungle. Villagers claimed the beast was a shy, harmless giant. In the Philippines, a "massive hairy creature" known as the Kapre was reported to be noxious smelling but unthreatening, and it reportedly maintained a rudimentary kind of trade agreement with local villagers. In the former Soviet Union, a creature called Snezhni Chelovyek inspired the formation of a government research program to investigate sightings during the 1950s, but the program was later abandoned. In Central Asia, close to the Yeti's home, the Alma is the local variant, which may simply be another name for the far-ranging Yeti. And in Africa, long held to

Photograph of an oversized footprint found in the snow-filled basins of Mount Everest. The footprint, measuring well over twelve inches, is believed by some to belong to the Yeti.

be the birthplace of all humanity, there is the Waterbobbejan, or "water baboon," of South Africa, and the Agogue, a more mischievous cousin, which has been spotted in Tanzania and along the Ivory Coast.

In all of these cases, the descriptions of the creature remain consistent: a tall, broad-shouldered creature, more ape than man yet walking upright. The rather pungent, or powerful, body odor also remains consistent, as does an apparent lack of speech; rare is the occasion when an ape-man is heard to utter a sound, much less anything that might be considered speech. Where these stories vary is in the level of contact they have with humans, from none at all to the nighttime trading of fruits and fish in exchange for cooked goods, as reported by villagers in Malaysia. Only rarely is the ape-being considered dangerous; more often than not, the only fatalities seem to involve a sheep or goat that wandered too far from the flock and shepherd. Even the few reports of violence done to humans would appear to stem more from the creature defending its home than from any warlike or aggressive instincts.

But all of this is conjecture, based on unsubstantiated stories, rumor, and legends. As Agent Scully of the eerie television show *The X-Files* might say to her partner, "Where is the evidence?"

Sightings and Evidence

The official record of Yeti sightings is a slim one. If you discount secondhand reports and stories that are closer to myth than fact, it becomes even less impressive. In fact, for such a widely known creature, there isn't much to base its existence on at all. Why is that?

First of all, we need to remember that for many, many years, the Himalayas were not easily accessible to outsiders. In part, this was because of the physical isolation, as discussed in the first chapter. The British did gain access during the nineteenth century thanks to their colonization of India. However, the trickle of British explorers never grew to a flood, and it soon ended.

But politics has been another problem. The borders of Nepal were closed in 1816, after the country lost a war with India, and they were not opened again officially until 1951. The British occupied Tibet in 1904, and maintained control until a treaty was signed the following year. China invaded Tibet in 1950, and since

The high-altitude Himalayas made hunting the Yeti very difficult.

then has occupied the small nation. From the beginning of the twentieth century until the end of World War II, it was almost impossible for any Westerner to enter the central Himalaya area legally. In fact, it wasn't until the 1950s that anyone was allowed back into the Himalaya Mountains, much less any scientific expeditions. And even then, the government could and did often require specific permissions that were very difficult to get. In fact, if you were to attempt to travel into Tibet today, you might find it impossible to get any sort of permission.

Yet with all these difficulties, some determined explorers did make their way into the mountains, even prior to 1950. But once they were actually on-site, why were they not able to gather more specific proof of the Yeti's existence?

First, remember the landscape. Ranging from 22,000 to 29,000 feet above sea level, the Himalaya Mountains are inhospitable to those not accustomed to high altitudes, making travel a slow, careful business. Winters are harsh, and spring brings with it the heavy rains known as monsoons, which can create flash floods and mudslides. One bad storm could wipe out half your party if you weren't ready for it.

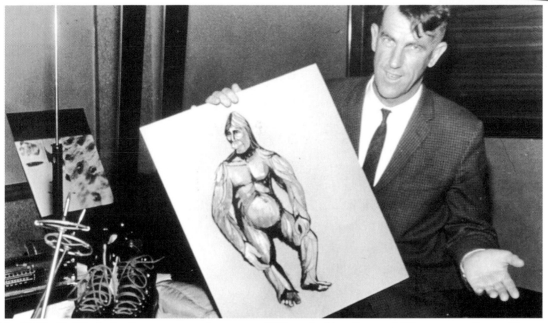

In 1960, World Book, Inc. sponsored an expedition, led by the world-famous explorer Sir Edmund Hillary *(above)* into the Himalaya Mountains to find scientific evidence of the Yeti.

Second, there's the technology. Prior to 1950, cameras were large, bulky, expensive machines that were difficult to work properly in extreme temperatures, assuming the delicate pieces made it safely up the mountainside. Unlike today's point-and-shoot cameras, those earlier models needed training to handle and proper conditions in order to get the best results. At the upper levels of Mount Everest, the air temperature can get dangerously cold, down to -20°C (-4°F). And the higher up you go, the colder and more bitterly dry the air becomes. It's not

Major Documented Yeti Sightings
1832–1950

1832 B. H. Hodson reports an attack on his native guides by creatures he referred to as "rakshas," or demons.

1889 Major L. A. Waddell reports finding large, bearlike footprints in the snow well above the elevation at which any bear should be living. His guides tell him it is a Yeti.

1913 A strange, very strong manlike creature covered in silvery yellow fur is reportedly captured by Chinese hunters. It dies after five months in captivity.

1921 An expedition led by Colonel C. K. Howard-Bury spots figures ahead of them while climbing Mount Everest. They find huge footprints of someone—or something—walking barefoot in the snowfield.

1923 Major Alan Cameron reports seeing figures along a cliff above the snowline. This time, photos are taken of footprints.

1925 N. A. Tombazi glimpses a creature ahead of him, some 15,000 feet up the side of Mount Everest.

1936 Footprints are found in the outer reaches of the snowline by the H. W. Tilman expedition.

1937 Explorer Frank Smythe reports finding tracks at the 14,000-foot level.

1948 A prospector by the name of Jan Frostis claims to have been attacked by Yetis, in one of the

rare physical encounters. His shoulder is
badly mangled.

1950   Mummified fingers and some skin are found
in the Himalayas. Experts determine that the
body parts are "almost human" but cannot
identify the species.

healthy for people and most certainly no good for film! For that reason, most of the historical evidence comes from written journals and sketches, with only the occasional black-and-white photograph of a footprint.

Modern expeditions, it might be assumed, would take with them modern equipment, allowing a much more accurate means to capture what proof they might find. This, however, is not often the case. While the technology has advanced, the cost for such tools has increased. And while the explorers of the previous century, and the scientists of the first half of the twentieth century, often had government backing to fund their supplies, the modern Yeti researchers all too often are working on a nonprofit basis, either on their own or through an organization that does not have the funds to outfit them properly. The exceptions, such as the Slick and the *Daily Mail* expeditions, will be discussed in the next chapter.

Investigations

Reading the accounts of past explorers searching for the Yeti, it may seem as though they went in without planning or preparation. Their expeditions seemed doomed to failure. But in the late 1950s, a series of organized explorations were launched after the Nepalese and Tibetan governments opened this borders to outsiders once again.

THE SHIPTON EXPEDITION AND PHOTOGRAPH

Eric Shipton was an experienced explorer, with half a dozen attempts to climb Mount Everest under his belt. In the winter of 1951, he and two companions were working their way across a neighboring mountain. They spotted a figure moving in the distance ahead of them, 20,000 feet up on the slopes of the Menlung Glacier. They tracked the Yeti until it disappeared into

Photographs showing large footprints--such as those above--of an unidentified creature are still the best evidence of the Yeti's existence.

an ice field. Shipton took a photograph of the creature's footprints. Those photos clearly showed the imprint of a foot that could have been that of a Yeti, an unknown animal, or a bear.

Photographed with an ice axe next to it, the clearest footprint measured twelve inches long by six inches wide. These footprints were not made by a human. The Shipton photograph is often held up as one of the best pieces of evidence of something living in the heights of the Himalayas.

OTHER MODERN EXPEDITIONS OF NOTE

The Daily Mail, a British newspaper, funded a survey in 1952. Zoologists, naturalists, cameramen, and trained guides formed the expedition. They found tracks and droppings, which they claimed came from a Yeti, plus a scalp of coarse hair unlike human hair. The expedition was allowed to take one hair from that scalp out of the country, but no more. Test results on its origin were inconclusive.

In 1954, American scientist Dr. Norman Dyrenfurth discovered caves in Kathmandu, Nepal, that showed evidence of having been inhabited by near-human creatures. He had plaster casts of footprints and hair samples as evidence. The results of testing on these samples at that time were inconclusive.

Between 1951 and 1953, Rene von Nebesky-Wojkowitz fielded several explorations as well. They found nothing but some tracks that didn't look like any known animal living in the area. Nebesky-Wojkowitz suggested that this failure was due to the Yeti's superior mobility over rough terrain and an increased lung capacity that gave it an impressive advantage in those high, oxygen-starved elevations.

THE SLICK EXPEDITIONS

In 1956, Thomas Slick, a Texas oilman and millionaire with a longtime interest in trying to discover the truth behind the Yeti legend, gained the backing of the San Antonio Zoo. Such sponsorship allowed Slick's party to enter the Himalayas as a legitimate, government-approved expedition. Thanks to Slick's money, the expedition came equipped with up-to-date scientific equipment, weapons, hounds to track the Yeti's scent, and enough men to cover a large area and question locals. Those interviews led

Slick to speculate that there were actually two or three different types of Yetis, each living in a different area of Tibet.

He and his crews made several trips into the mountains, coming back with photos, footprint castings, and—in a rather brazen act of smuggling that involved the aid of American actor James Stewart and his wife—two fingers from a mummified hand that locals claimed was that of a Yeti. Called the Pangboche hand for the location it was taken from, Slick's team replaced the stolen fingers with human ones so their theft would not be quickly noticed, then slipped the mummified digits into the luggage of the Stewarts, trusting that the luggage of such world-famous people would not be searched.

The Stewarts arrived safely in London, but their luggage didn't! It was lost between flights, and the scientists had to assume that even if the luggage was found, their prized piece of evidence would be discovered and confiscated. However, the luggage was returned to the Stewarts soon after, still unsearched.

So what happened to all this evidence? No one is quite sure. Loren Coleman, in his book *Tom Slick and the Search for the Yeti,* mentions that a footprint cast and hair were reportedly sent to *Life* magazine, which had been "consulting" with Slick on his discoveries. It may be that they are still stored somewhere in a warehouse, unmarked and forgotten.

THE HILLARY REBUTTAL

The Slick expeditions should have been enough to make the search for the Yeti a reputable scientific venture. But Sir Edmund Hillary, world famous as the first Westerner to climb Mount Everest, was determined to debunk the Yeti myth once and for all.

In 1960, a scientific expedition sponsored by World Book, Inc., went into the Himalayas, led by Sir Edmund Hillary and Marlin Perkins, who would in later years star in the nature documentary series *Wild Kingdom.* During their three months in the field, they investigated the "proof" Slick's team claimed to have found. And it was here that the Pangboche hand came back to haunt Thomas Slick. With the human fingers added, its veracity—along with that of other pelts and scalps—was thrown into serious doubt. In addition, Hillary publicly disputed the words

Sir Edmund Hillary *(left)*, world famous for leading the first Western expedition to climb Mount Everest, was passionate about finding the truth behind the Yeti legend.

of his former guide, the Sherpa, Sen Tensing, saying, "He . . . had been attending the three-day Mani Rimdu ceremony . . . one that I knew by experience ended in a carnival atmosphere with much drinking of beer and spirits."

In other words, Sen Tensing was an unreliable witness because he was in a location where alcohol was being consumed. There was no evidence that Sen Tensing himself had been drinking or was in any way incapacitated, but the implication, from such a respected figure, was enough. The World Book expedition's report that the Yeti was nothing more than a myth was more newsworthy than Slick's claims to the contrary, and they had the weight of public opinion on their side, including articles in *Life* and *National Geographic,* among others, and a traveling road show in the mid 1960s featuring Perkins and Hillary.

AN INCIDENTAL FIND

In 1970, an expedition not related to hunting the Yeti, on the south face of Annapurna (the tenth highest mountain in the world, also located in the Himalayas), found a series of footprints in areas known to have no human habitation, and no known population of large animals such as bears. The leader of the expedition, Don Whillans, reported tracking a humanoid creature for about twenty minutes before losing sight of it.

But by the 1970s, the wave of public opinion had turned. The hunt for the Yeti had been recast from scientific exploration to the foolishness of crackpots.

Science Responds

The evidence presented in defense of the existence of the Yeti has been, at best, sketchy. Reported sightings, blurred photographs, casts of footprints that may or may not have been created by known, documented animals such as bears, or the possibility of an outright hoax, have not helped to prove the Yeti's existence. The few unidentified pieces of physical evidence are just dubious enough for them to be justifiably dismissed from consideration by the rational eye of a skeptic.

The urge, in fact, is often to dismiss Yeti sightings the same way many scientists dismiss UFO sightings or the existence of the Loch Ness monster. The pursuit of truth would be much easier if we could just write off every person who saw a distorted footprint in the snow or caught a glimpse of what might have been an upright, manlike figure lumbering off into the distance. But the mark of a true scientist is one who doesn't discard any theory or claim, no matter how crazy it may sound, until it has been proven untrue. Many of the scientific findings we now take as self-evident—fossils, for example—were once held to be hoaxes or mistaken identifications. Lack of proof cannot be taken as proof of nonexistence. It is for those reasons that science has not yet been able to close the books on the Yeti.

Yes, all the sightings might just be the result of hallucinations caused by the high altitude and resulting lack of oxygen, or charlatans looking to pull a scam and make money off of their celebrity. But what of those footprints, the unidentifiable droppings and hairs, the photographs and videotapes of footprints, the long history of consistent reporting by many people? Is it possible that the Yeti, rather than simply being a figment of our imaginations, is actually an identifiable, natural part of our world?

THE THEORIES

Some researchers claim that the Yeti and its kin around the world are "wild men," perhaps direct descendents of the first primates to come out of Africa, and evolved to an intelligence near to that of ours. Others think that the Yeti is a modern but not yet identified ape, a closer relative to the gorilla than to humans. But one of the

A partial skull of an early hominid, our closest evolutionary ancestor

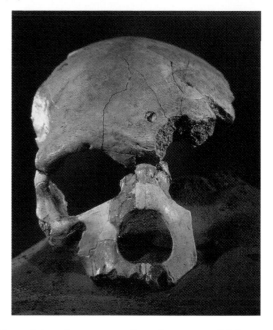

most plausible scenarios offered to date involves Gigantopithecus.

Gigantopithecus was the largest primate to live on Earth. It stood almost ten feet high and weighed close to 600 pounds. This great ape lived during the Pleistocene era, 1.8 million to 10,000 years ago. The fossil record from that time shows that it lived in the area that is now China and Southeast Asia.

According to scientists, Gigantopithecus looked very much like today's gorilla, not walking upright on two feet, but using arms and knuckles to cover ground more efficiently on four limbs. Fossil records also suggest that its dietary habits were much the same as its modern descendants—mostly vegetarian. If so, we can assume that its behavior might also mimic that of modern gorillas: shy and retiring creatures that nonetheless can become quite aggressive when threatened.

There are enough similarities in appearance and overlap in territory that the link between the Yeti and Gigantopithecus cannot be dismissed out of hand. Is it possible that a branch of this ancient family did not die out some 500,000 years ago, as always thought?

Since there is no obvious reason why Gigantopithecus became extinct, save for a probable failure to adapt to changes in the climate during the Ice Age, it is possible that such a branch does exist. Certainly the remoteness of the region would aid such a race in remaining undiscovered until only recently. This would explain the scant reports of such creatures until the nineteenth century.

The arguments against this theory are that Gigantopithecus theoretically stood between eight and ten feet tall, while the Yeti reportedly average five feet tall—barely the size of an adult human. It is possible that the species might have shrunk, but such a great difference between those average heights makes this seem unlikely.

Other researchers claim that the Yeti might be a descendant of our own ancestor, the Neanderthal. The height would certainly be a better match, but the reported hairiness of the Yeti gives pause: Neanderthals would have been no hairier than an average Homo sapien, or modern human.

An artist's representation of a tribe of Neanderthals. Some scientists hypothesize that the Yeti may be the modern descendent of an earlier primate, such as Gigantopithecus.

Both these theories take a heavy blow when faced with the fact that the last Neanderthal has been dated at 40,000 BC, and Gigantopithecus was last seen in the fossil record at 500,000 years BC. Without more recent fossil records, it is almost impossible to draw a connection that will stand up to scientific scrutiny.

ANOTHER BRANCH IN OUR FAMILY TREE?

A recent report in the *New York Times* has cast all previous explanations into doubt. In 1999, a group of paleontologists led by Dr. Maeve Leakey found a skull in northern Kenya, in Africa. After careful study, it was determined that the nearly complete skull was 3.5 million years old and belonged to a completely different genus and species than they had expected. Whereas before, scientists thought that modern Homo sapiens had descended from Lucy (*Australopithecus afarensis*), the fossil species that dated back 3.5 to 4 million years, it now may be that our family tree has a great many branches—and the founding parent of our own specific branch is in doubt. And if this is the case, then who is to say that the Yeti cannot exist—and in fact, may be a cousin of ours, descended from a 3 million year old branch?

According to Dr. Leakey, when hominids split off from the great apes and began walking upright, it would make sense that they would wander into different territories and adapt to their new homes. If one of these offshoot branches were to have wandered from Africa into the highlands of Asia, it would certainly have developed a coat of hair to protect itself from the cold, larger feet, like a snowshoe rabbit, to run along the surface of the snow, and many other characteristics that could describe the Yeti.

In short, just when we think science has given us an answer, new discoveries cast light on old evidence and make us question again our previous conclusions.

Future Investigations

What all of the reports prove is that there is no proof, one way or the other, to decide the Yeti question once and for all. If you choose to believe in the Yeti, the evidence seems beyond any doubt. If you choose to be skeptical, the stories are flimsy and the evidence is unreliable.

However, there is still the possibility that, in the not too distant future, science will be able to conclusively prove the existence—or nonexistence—of the Yeti. With the fine-tuning of such technology as spectrographics (the ability to find objects or individuals through the heat they generate naturally) and spy satellites, we may soon be able to determine if any man-sized creatures live in the heights of the Himalayas.

But it's not enough to simply discover if something lives there. A heat signature of that size might be a bear or a reclusive human.

We need to identify what it is that lives out there. All we need is to retrieve new, uncontaminated samples of alleged Yeti skin or hair.

The announced completion of the genome project, giving us a blueprint of the human genetic structure, has given us another instrument to use in the search for the Yeti. Unlike previous testing, we would now be able to break down the genetic structure of a hair sample, for example, and compare it to all known genetic samples. And when that happens, we will have a much better idea of how close to Homo sapiens this mysterious creature is—if it is at all.

But perhaps rather than *when,* it should be *if* we retrieve new samples. The Yeti has proven elusive for many years, and in recent years the Chinese government took down an offered bounty payable on evidence of the Yeti, perhaps fearing a repeat of what happened with the giant panda, or worse, the total destruction of the creature's habitat that might lead to its inevitable extinction. Unlike the explorers of the nineteenth and early twentieth centuries, we understand the delicate balance of nature, even if we don't always work within it. It may be that, like the giant panda, the Yeti is slow to breed and slow to recover from human incursions. It is possible that, like so many other

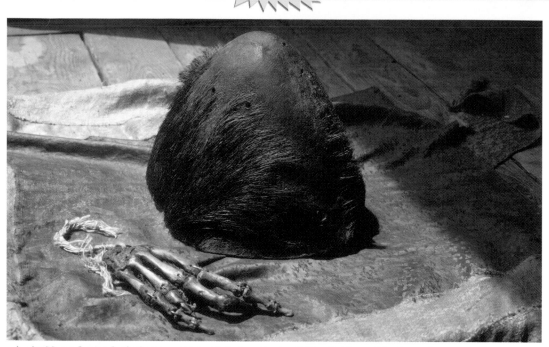

A skull and hand skeleton rumored to be that of the Yeti on display at a monastery located near Mount Everest. Solid evidence of Yeti's existence has not yet been found.

animals discovered postextinction, they have already died out and that the scraps we have are all that remains.

Or it may be that the Yeti has outsmarted us in our fumblings to find physical evidence of its existence. After avoiding contact with humans for hundreds of years, thriving in an otherwise inhospitable location, perhaps the Yeti has also perfected the art of concealment, remaining one step ahead of those who would capture it. The Yeti has remained a myth for thousands of years, after all, despite man's most determined efforts. Perhaps it will always remain so.

Glossary

Bigfoot   The North American version of the Yeti, frequently spotted along the U.S./Canadian border, especially in Washington State.

Buddhism   A religion and philosophy founded in India around 525 BC by Siddhartha Gautama, who was called the Buddha. There are over 300 million Buddhists worldwide.

Gigantopithecus   An extinct ape dating back more than 500,000 years; the largest primate yet discovered.

glacier   A mass of ice typically found in extremely cold climates such as Alaska, formed by snow that is compressed into granular ice. Glaciers move at a slow pace, pushed forward by gravity and their own weight.

Himalayas   One of the greatest mountain ranges in the entire world, reaching from Pakistan through India, to Tibet and Nepal.

Hinduism   One of the oldest living religions in the world, practiced by the majority of the people of India.

hominid   Humans and their primate ancestors.

Homo sapien   The species, or categorization, to which contemporary humans belong.

Neanderthal   An ancient subspecies of Homo sapiens.

Pleistocene era   A time period in the earth's history, which began roughly 1.8 million years ago and ended 11,000 years ago, during which much of the world was covered by water and/or ice.

primate   An animal in the order primates, which includes apes, monkeys, lemurs, and humans.

Sherpa   A people living in Nepal who have a reputation for being the best mountain climbers and guides in the world.

Yeti   The common name given to the two-legged creature frequently spotted in the far reaches of Nepal and Tibet.

For More Information

ORGANIZATIONS

The Bigfoot Field Researchers Organization
Web site: http://www.bfro.net/

International Society of Cryptozoology
P.O. Box 43070
Tucson, AZ 85733
(520) 884-8369
e-mail: iscz@azstarnet.com
Web site: http://perso.wanadoo.fr/cryptozoo/associations/asso_eng.htm

WEB SITES

Due to the changing nature of Internet links, the Rosen Publishing Group, Inc., has developed an online list of Web sites related to the subject of this book. This site is updated regularly. Please use this link to access the list:

http://www.rosenlinks.com/um/yeti

For Further Reading

Cohen, Daniel. *Monster Hunting Today.* New York: Penguin Putnam, 1983.

Coleman, Loren. *Tom Slick and the Search for the Yeti.* London: Faber & Faber, 1989.

Coleman, Loren, and Jerome Clarke. *Cryptozoology A to Z: The Encyclopedia of Loch Monsters, Sasquatch, Chupacabras, and Other Authentic Mysteries of Nature.* New York: Simon & Schuster, 1999.

Coleman, Loren, and Patrick Huyghe. *The Field Guide to Bigfoot, Yeti, and Other Mystery Primates Worldwide.* New York: Worldwide Avon Books, 1999.

Heuvelmans, Bernard. *On the Track of Unknown Animals.* New York: Columbia University Press, 1995

Tchernine, Odette. *In Pursuit of the Abominable Snowman.* New York: Taplinger Publishing, 1971.

"In Search of the Yeti," *Fortean Times,* Issue 67, 1994.

Index

ABOUT THE AUTHOR

Laura Anne Gilman lives in New Jersey with her husband, Peter, and her cat, Pandora.

PHOTO CREDITS

Cover © Anna Zuckerman-Vdovenko/Index Stock; p. 4 illustration by Thomas Forget; p. 7 © Liaison; p. 13 © Alison Wright/Corbis; p. 16 © Corbis; pp. 18, 27 © Hulton-Deutsch Collection/Corbis; p. 21 © Papilio/ Corbis; p. 23 © Popperfoto/Archive Photos by Getty Images; p. 32 © Hulton/Archive Photos by Getty Images; p. 36 © *National Geographic*; p. 38 © Mansell/TimePix; p. 42 © Ernst Haas/Hulton/Archive Photos by Getty Images.

SERIES DESIGN AND LAYOUT

Geri Giordano